11 Daytona Beach
Community College
dbcc

Daytona Beach Community College

Fifty Years of Shaping Our Community

By Charles Carroll

THE
DONNING COMPANY
PUBLISHERS

The Donning Company Publishers
184 Business Park Drive, Suite 206
Virginia Beach, VA 23462–6533

Steve Mull, General Manager
Barbara Buchanan, Office Manager
Ashley Campbell and Heather Floyd, Editors
Todd Aftel, Graphic Designer
Derek Eley, Imaging Artist
Scott Rule, Director of Marketing
Lynn Walton, Project Research Coordinator

B. L. Walton Jr., Project Director

Library of Congress Cataloging-in-Publication Data

Carroll, Charles, 1949-
  Daytona Beach Community College: fifty years of shaping our community / by Charles Carroll.
    p. cm.
  ISBN-13: 978-1-57864-442-1
  1. Daytona Beach Community College (Fla.)--History. 2. Daytona Beach Junior College (Fla.)--History. I. Title.
  LD6501.D39C37 2007
    378.759'21--dc22
                        2007024444

Printed in the United States of America by Walsworth Publishing Company

Table of Contents

Message from the President   4

Prologue   Opportunity Knocks   6

1. A Matter of Time   Two Colleges Are Born   8

2. New Frontiers   First Steps on the Educational Journey   12

3. The Late 1960s   Changing Times, New Buildings, and a Merger   22

4. Coming of Age   The 1970s and '80s   28

5. Winds of Change   Beyond Bricks and Mortar: The 1990s   48

6. Daytona Beach Community College   A Pictorial View   62

7. Stepping Into the Future   Milestones and Indicators of Excellence   94

8. A New Century   100

9. The Evolution Continues   114

Appendix   118

Index   124

Author Biography   128

Message from the President

Fifty years ago, a group of progressive citizens in Volusia and Flagler Counties had a vision. That vision was destined to forever change the role that education would play in the development of these two east central Florida counties. Today, fifty years later, the reality of the vision is evident throughout the region, the state, and even the nation. Daytona Beach Community College, the institution that emerged from that vision, has impacted millions of lives and contributed significantly to the region's economic and cultural development. At the fiftieth milestone, the College is still young at heart but seasoned in its ability to deliver programs and services to the citizens who have come to expect nothing less than excellence.

Fittingly, as the College celebrates this special milestone, it is also blazing new trails that promise to make the future as equally dynamic as the first fifty years. In May 2007, forty-seven years after graduating its first class with associate degrees, the College graduated its first class with baccalaureate degrees. While keeping its mission of serving Volusia and Flagler residents in focus, the College, having served international students from over fifty countries for many years, is now reaching out to schools in the Bahamas and Dominican Republic to assist these countries in developing their own community college systems.

As the following pages will illustrate, the Daytona Beach Community College at the fiftieth-year juncture is significantly different than it was at its inception. Certainly, that difference will become even more profound as we move forward into the future.

D. Kent Sharples, President
Daytona Beach Community College

Prologue Opportunity Knocks

The Opportunity School opened in 1929 on the cusp of a global depression that would plunge the world into another war. It was an apt name for a school that taught commercial and business skills to those who couldn't go to college.

Funded by the Smith-Hughes Act, the school changed names (during the war years through 1945, the school was known as Volusia County Vocational School and trained hundreds of people as war-production workers) and locations over two decades, moving from various buildings and rented rooms in downtown Daytona Beach to a permanent site on Welch Boulevard, across from Mainland High School. But the Opportunity School never lost sight of its mission or even the meaning of its name—giving young adults hope that vocational education and training opened doors to a better life.

Mary Brennan Karl: An early visionary who saw the importance of education to the area, Mrs. Karl was named the director of the Opportunity School in 1937. The school later became the known as the Mary Karl Vocational School and was the forerunner of Daytona Beach Community College. (Source: DBCC Archives)

Mary Brennan Karl, a commercial teacher for the Daytona Beach School System, was named director of the Opportunity School in 1937. Karl's tenacious determination became a driving force behind the school, which later evolved into the Mary Karl Vocational School. The Mary Karl Vocational School eventually became the technical division of the new Daytona Beach Junior College.

Thus, over the course of almost eighty years, first the Opportunity School, then the Mary Karl Vocational School began an educational journey that is now the Daytona Beach Community College (DBCC) that we know today. The College is about to turn fifty, a seminal moment in itself. But when the anniversary marks the evolution of an institution that truly has made a difference in the lives of nearly everyone it's touched, the anniversary should be celebrated with more than a spectacular party.

Daytona Beach Community College: Fifty Years of Shaping Our Community is not just a recitation and reflection of history and facts, impressive as they are; it is instead a record of the evolution of an idea. From its inception, the value of DBCC has been its human spirit and human touch. This book is a living testimony told through the images of DBCC's founders, students, faculty, staff, alumni, presidents, trustees, and community, and the events in which they participated.

When the final photo is viewed and the last page turned, what remains is a salute to the achievements, no matter how big or small, of those inextricably linked to Daytona Beach Community College—at heart, an institution of opportunity for all who enter.

Background: Community Colleges in Florida

Florida's first public community college was established in Palm Beach in 1933. Palm Beach Junior College remained as the lone public two-year college in the state until 1947. In 1947, the Florida Citizens Committee on Education developed a report to the Florida legislature. The junior college section of the report was assigned to Howell Watkins, the principal of Palm Beach High School and dean of Palm Beach Junior College. Watkins assigned the task to a graduate of Palm Beach Community College who was currently a graduate student at the University of Florida. From that point forward, the student, James Wattenbarger, played a significant role in the development of Florida's community college system. In fact, he has often been referred to as the Father of Florida's Community College System.

The 1947 report resulted in the passage of the Minimum Foundation Program. This report led to a series of additional events and studies, including the University of Florida Press's first education-oriented book, *A State Plan for Public Junior Colleges,* by Dr. James L. Wattenbarger in 1953. Also in 1953, the legislature established the Board of Control, which was the forerunner to the Board of Regents. In 1955, the Council for the Study of Higher Education, under the direction of the Board of Control, issued its first report to the legislature calling for conducting a separate study for junior colleges in Florida. Dr. Wattenbarger was granted a leave of absence from the University of Florida to direct the study. The report was accepted in 1957 and approved, establishing six new colleges. Daytona Beach Junior College was among the six newly authorized colleges.

Also of significant importance was the concurrent authorization of Volusia County Community College to serve the area's black citizens. Thus, a parallel journey had begun—one that would eventually merge and result in today's Daytona Beach Community College.

Notwithstanding the unique challenges that Volusia County Community College and its sister institutions faced, the entire two-year college system faced an uphill battle to take its rightful place in the educational delivery spectrum.

Fifty years later, many thousands of Florida citizens have graduated from the academic and technical programs offered by two-year colleges and are contributing to the state's economic growth. Yet, many in the state still treat the system as a junior, rather than an equal, partner in higher education and key player in economic development.

Daytona Beach Community College: Fifty Years of Shaping Our Community chronicles the development and growth of two colleges. In 1958, Daytona Beach Junior College and Volusia County Community College began as separate institutions, but in 1966, they merged into one institution—Daytona Beach Junior College. In 1971, Daytona Beach Junior College became Daytona Beach Community College. Through a merger and name change, the concept of a college serving its community remained strong and has become a reality in the form of an institution that daily shapes the Volusia and Flagler communities. As Daytona Beach Community College enters its fiftieth year, it has moved to a four-year status with authorization from both the state and the regional accrediting agencies to offer its first four-year degree. Just as its roots stemmed from an idea in the minds of progressive citizens, its evolution has been shaped by the same kind of progressive thinking.

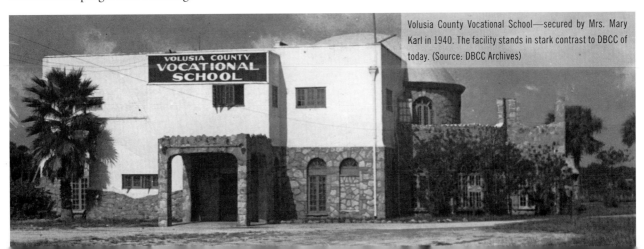

Volusia County Vocational School—secured by Mrs. Mary Karl in 1940. The facility stands in stark contrast to DBCC of today. (Source: DBCC Archives)

Chapter 1

A Matter of Time

Two Colleges Are Born

Headlines in a 1948 *Daytona Beach News-Journal* edition read, "Welch School given to County/Future use as Junior College Seen." It was a bold, visionary statement that gave wings to an aggressive grassroots effort that eventually brought Florida's pilot comprehensive community college to "The World's Most Famous Beach." Twenty-nine acres and fifty-five buildings of the Welch Center were turned over to Volusia County from the War Assets Administration in the exchange. The War Assets Administration had used the site as an army convalescent and rehabilitation center during World War II.

Starting in 1946, through the efforts of Mary Brennan Karl and her contacts in Washington, D.C., approval was obtained to allow several programs of the Mary Karl Vocational School to operate on the site on an interim-use basis. This approval was followed by a restricted deed of the property to the Volusia County School Board in 1948 and the headline announcing the future development of a college on the site.

A small group of public school officials, citizens, and the Volusia County Continuing Council on Education understood the value of offering convenient, affordable education, training, and enrichment programs to Volusia/Flagler County citizens. Today, it is popularly called "intellectual capital." Back then, these leaders, educators, and average citizens simply knew the value of education in a community's quality of life. Recognizing this value, County Director of Education A. F. Edmunds stated, "No school in Florida except ours can present a college program that's really for the community. We will serve the needs of youngsters out of high school all the way up to retired persons in their 90s or older." The reality of this statement was documented in 2002, when Dr. Kent Sharples, the seventh president of the current Daytona Beach Community College, bestowed a high school diploma upon Harry Patrinelli, a ninety-year-old who had returned to school to earn his diploma in order to obtain his real estate license.

The land gift in 1948 set the stage for a series of events that took place over the next decade and culminated in 1957 with the establishment of Daytona Beach Junior College (DBJC). This outcome was made possible by several intervening events. The 1955 Florida legislature established the Community College Council and charged it with the responsibility of developing a long-range expansion of the community junior colleges in the state. Also in 1955, the Volusia County Continuing Council of Education was organized to intensify the efforts to obtain a college for the Volusia County area. Through surveys, questionnaires, population studies, speaker's bureaus, and media publicity, the local council documented and solidified the need for access to college-level education for the area's citizens. The plan developed by the council called for a college to serve Volusia and Flagler Counties. In keeping with the segregated status of education at that time, a second junior college, located in Daytona Beach, was planned to serve the area's black population.

On March 4, 1957, John H. Smiley, superintendent of Volusia County Schools, submitted to James L. Wattenbarger, director of Florida's Community College Council, certified copies of a series of resolutions passed by the board.

Dr. James M. Snyder, the first president of Daytona Beach Junior College. (Source: DBCC yearbook)

These resolutions were the formal beginning of the application to establish a junior college in Volusia County. Volusia County's resolution was followed by a similar one from the Flagler County Board of Public Instruction.

Wattenbarger responded with a letter describing the process for forming an advisory committee for the junior college. He indicated that these appointments must be made by the time the state board gave its official approval for the organization of the college. Since the college was intended to serve two counties, Wattenbarger explained that the county of location (Volusia) would get five members and Flagler would get four members.

A. F. Edmunds, director of education for Volusia County Schools, was authorized to serve as coordinator in the Community Junior College Study for the Volusia/Flagler area. The Florida Community College Council was to make its final recommendations to the State Board of Education before the 1957 session of the Florida legislature. As part of its investigation, the state council established fourteen areas in Florida, including thirty-two counties, to be placed in a category called Priority Group One. The 1957 legislature's goal was to establish five junior colleges from this list.

Volusia and Flagler Counties were included in one of the fourteen areas under consideration. The State Board of Education approved the establishment of the junior college on April 9, 1957, noting that the "brief prepared by the local Council [Volusia and Flagler Counties] was one of the best presented to the state Community College Council." The approval also noted that 4,507 individuals were expected to be served during the first year of operation. Of that number, almost 1,000 were expected to be taking university transfer-level courses, while the remainder would be involved in adult and vocational courses. The 1957 legislature appropriated funds for operations and capital outlay. The College was approved as the state's pilot comprehensive community college offering the first two years of a four-year degree, vocational training, and adult education. The school's official name would become Daytona Beach Junior College.

Volusia County Community College

In parallel fashion, as Daytona Beach Junior College was being developed, Volusia County Community College (VCCC) was also being developed. VCCC was one of twelve district black colleges developed to serve Florida's black citizens.

Like DBJC, VCCC grew out of the Florida legislature's enactment of the Minimum Foundation Program. The program, Florida's first major effort to establish educational standards, was designed to assure educational opportunities to everyone from children in elementary school to college level students. This same act changed the Florida State College for Women to the co-educational Florida State University and opened the University of Florida to female students for the first time.

VCCC was governed by the Volusia County Board of Public Instruction with input from a college advisory committee.

Chapter 2

New Frontiers

First Steps on the Educational Journey

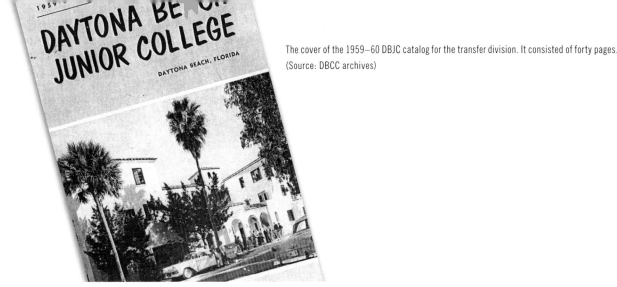

The cover of the 1959–60 DBJC catalog for the transfer division. It consisted of forty pages. (Source: DBCC archives)

Daytona Beach Junior College would be part of the Volusia County School System. The Mary Karl Vocational School already offered programs on the Welch site, some in former army barracks. This "hybrid" institution—college transfer and vocational—had much work to do in order to be ready for the first freshman class, which would enroll in September 1958.

A new college needed a president to take the helm and lead this new endeavor through the uncharted waters of turning a fledging initiative into a true institution of higher learning. Dr. James M. Snyder was chosen from more than forty applicants to carry out this task, serving as president of DBJC from January 1, 1958, to June 30, 1960.

Dr. Snyder's starting salary was $9,000. Prior to coming to DBJC, he served as vice president and dean of instruction at Sinclair College in Dayton, Ohio. He held a doctorate from the University of Cincinnati and had extensive experience in vocational and industrial education. After leaving DBJC in 1960 and before his retirement, Dr. Snyder held positions at Muskegon, Michigan, Phoenix, Arizona, and Central Illinois.

QUOTE FROM DR. SNYDER when leaving DBJC:

"I feel that it has been a great privilege to have had the opportunity of starting the new junior college program at Daytona Beach. Further, I am proud of both the program and the faculty in the college transfer division for there is evidence that this program rates among the top of all these in the state. This fact is remarkable when it is realized that we are only in our second year of operation and other programs in the state range in age up to twenty-six years."

Source: DBCC "Twenty-Year Report: 1957–77."

For its 1958 opening, the college was organized into three divisions: Adult Education, College Transfer, and Vocational-Technical. A budget of $37,666 was available for purchase of teaching and office supplies.

One of the first tasks for the newly approved junior college was to secure a physical location for classes. A logical place to look was the Mary Karl Vocational School that was already established on a twenty-nine-acre tract located near Halifax Hospital and owned by the school. The site was able to serve the technical students with makeshift accommodations; however, it did not have adequate physical space to house all of the new transfer division of the college. Thus, it became necessary to rent space in the Princess Issena Hotel Inn, located two blocks from the beach, for two years.

The 1958–59 College Transfer Division catalog listed four programs of study:
- Associate Degree Program leading toward a Bachelor of Arts Degree

Above: Dr. Roy Bergengren (at podium), early in his tenure as president (1960–74) honors Mary Karl (portrait in front of podium) during Mary Karl Day. Mayor Eubank of Daytona Beach first commemorated Mary Karl Day via proclamation on November 2, 1959. (Seated left to right) Dr. Hal Massey, vice president of academic affairs; Representative Fred Karl; Jeanne Goddard, member of the Volusia County School Board; and John Smiley, Volusia County Schools superintendent. (Source: DBCC archives)
Right: Dr. Roy Bergengren, DBJC's second president. (Source: DBCC archives)

- Associate Degree Program leading toward a Bachelor's Degree in Science or Engineering

- Associate Degree Program leading toward a Bachelor's Degree in Business Administration

- Associate Degree Program leading toward a Bachelor's Degree in an area not specifically listed in this catalog.

The catalog was a twelve-page typed document. The copy available for this research did not list the College's administration or faculty.

The new college enjoyed widespread support in the local community. Scholarship donations from area organizations began immediately, among them the Daytona Beach Emblem Club, Carpenter's Local 1725, and PEO Sisterhood. Among the early individual contributors were Dr. and Mrs. Eric Lenholt. Today, the student center at the Daytona Beach Campus is named the Lenholt Student Center.

After Dr. Snyder's departure at the end of June 1960, Dr. N. B. McMillian served as acting president for a brief stint prior to Dr. Roy F. Bergengren assuming the college's presidency in August 1960. Dr. McMillian was one of the college's first employees and was serving as dean of the Transfer Division when he was tapped to serve as interim president upon Dr. Snyder's departure. Dr. Bergengren served as president for fourteen years, until May 1974.

During his fourteen years of service to Daytona Beach Community College, Dr. Bergengren oversaw many milestones, including construction of many of the campus's early buildings and the initial accreditation with the Southern Association

of Colleges and Schools. He also played a major role in the merger between Volusia County Community College and Daytona Beach Junior College. He was in office during the change in administrative responsibility from the public school system to the District Board of Trustees and the college's name change from Daytona Beach Junior College to Daytona Beach Community College in July 1971.

In a statement released upon his retirement as president, Dr. Bergengren said, "I see the biggest problems facing community colleges in this decade [1970s] are seeking out new programs to serve the community, finance for occupational programs and curricula improvement." This statement set the initiative for the incoming president.

Volusia County Community College

The first and only president of Volusia County Community College was J. Griffen Greene. Born in 1910, Mr. Greene earned a bachelor's degree from Knoxville College, a master's from Atlanta University, and completed further study at Yale University and the University of Michigan.

Commenting on the need to establish Volusia Community College, President Greene said there were two factors: "First, was the desire on the part of many high school students to go on to a four-year college upon graduation. However, most of the students were without the finances to pay for most of the cost of matriculating at the institutions located elsewhere. Second, Cape Canaveral and the Kennedy Space Center were requiring great numbers of carpenters, block and brick layers, as well as technicians." (Source: Smith, Walter L., *The Magnificent Twelve: Florida's Black Junior Colleges.* Winter Park, FL: Four-G Publishers Inc., 1994.)

President Greene, along with his faculty and staff, aggressively sought to fulfill the desires and needs of the students with whom he was entrusted to educate. Volusia County Community College quickly took its place, not only as an educational institution, but also as a major community resource in the black community of Daytona Beach.

The Students and First Yearbook

The first students were area high school seniors who were taking a bold step—going to college—but, unlike many of their friends, not going away, since there were new local institutions available to serve them. A glimpse of

President J. Griffen Greene, the first and only president of Volusia County Community College. (Source: DBCC archives)

the first students is provided through the first yearbook.

Daytona Beach Junior College, like any new institution, needed to establish its identity and traditions. A new college needed a yearbook. Inspired by the location of classes for the transfer division, the Issena Hotel, the first yearbook was called the *InnKeeper*.

Produced during the spring of 1959, the *InnKeeper* consisted of ninety-two pages. An insight into the students' thinking during that first year is captured in the yearbook's dedication: "We gratefully dedicate this first Annual of the Daytona Beach Junior College to all those men and women who so generously gave their time and talents to pioneer the paths so these college doors could open."

The editor was one of the bright new students who took advantage of the new local educational opportunity, Marvin Wade "Skip" Lowery. To Lowery, in his own words, "The junior college was a savior. If it had not opened when it did, I was headed to the Army." After his two years at DBJC, Lowery transferred to Florida State University and eventually returned to DBJC to teach humanities. He retired in 1998 but continued to teach on a part-time basis.

Richard Bruner "Rich" Rosier was another enrollee at DBJC in its first class. Rosier, whose intent was to attend law school, had already attended the University of Florida for a semester but decided to return home after experiencing financial difficulties. According to Rosier, "DBJC was the greatest thing in the world." Rosier became the first president of the Student Government Association. After gradating from DBJC, he transferred to Stetson University, earned a bachelor of laws degree, and established a successful law practice in Daytona Beach. Rosier later served on the college's Board of Trustees.

Lowery and Rosier were just two of 101 sophomores featured in the second (1960) edition of the *InnKeeper*. According to data in the yearbook, the fall 1959 enrollment brought the total enrollment in the transfer division to over 800 students.

The First Buildings

By 1960, the *InnKeeper* had grown to 130 pages. Skip Lowery continued as editor, along with Judy McNeil as co-editor. Although the *InnKeeper* name was retained, the 1960 yearbook celebrated the opening of the college's first permanent building on October 20, 1959. The building, called the Science Building, later called Building One and currently labeled Building 340, is still in existence and now houses language laboratories and the Instructional Television System, a two-way audio and video technology that allows instruction originating at one campus to be broadcast in real time to all other campuses. The 1960 yearbook contained the following commentary on the opening of the new building: "On

Attorney Richard Rosier, DBJC's first SGA president. He graduated in the first class, and after attending law school, became a trustee. (Source: DBCC archives)

October 20th, after several construction delays, the Junior College opened the doors of the new science building and began the first classes to be held on the Welch campus. Compared to the makeshift atmosphere of the Inn the modern educational facilities were an inspiration to students and faculty alike." In a less serious commentary, several students were quoted as saying, "Yeah, it's beautiful and all that, but what about some heat?" and "Now I guess there's no excuse for not learning something."

With the opening of the Science Building, DBJC was clearly on its way to establishing a lasting presence in the area. Buildings continued to rise, and many of them were named for prominent citizens and others who played various roles in building the college and the community.

The Science Building was just the beginning of the on-going facility development process on the Daytona Campus that is still underway. Significant detail is available for some of the building projects, while little detail is available for others. Brief summaries and photographs of some the campus building initiatives on the Daytona and other campuses are included throughout this book. Initially, all college buildings were numbered in the sequence in which they were built. By the 1990s, the Daytona Campus had become so large that a sequential numbering system was impractical. The buildings are numbered in grouped, structured fashion.

Within ten years of its 1959 opening, the campus had six major buildings, including the original science building, a library, an administration building, two classroom/ technology buildings, and a student center.

On the administrative and academic side, the early 1960s brought much change to the new and rapidly growing Daytona Beach

Paul Baker, labor leader and Board of Trustees chair from Holly Hill, in front of Baker Hall, which was completed in 1968. (Source: DBCC archives)

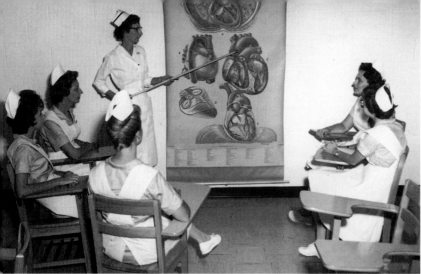

Junior College. The following are some of the highlights for the 1962–63 and 1963–64 academic years:

- DBJC received state of Florida accreditation on May 2, 1962, clearing the way for applying for regional accreditation to the Southern Association. The regional accreditation application was accepted and approved in November 1962 at the association's meeting in Dallas, Texas. An on-site visit was scheduled for March 13–15, 1963. The committee's recommendation was highly favorable, and the association granted the college its initial full regional accreditation.

- DBCC, now fully accredited, rapidly moved ahead toward developing new programs and serving the community. Some key milestones included the following:

  - The associate degree nursing program accepted its first class of 47 students in fall 1962. During spring 1964, 24 nursing students graduated.
  - A cooperative hotel-motel management program enrolled its first students in fall 1964.
  - The college offered its first credit course by television in 1962–63 in cooperation with WESH-TV.
  - The Civil Technology program enrolled its first students in fall 1963.
  - In cooperation with Halifax Hospital, the surgical technical assistant program graduated its first class at the end of the 1963–64 year.

During fall 1964, the college adopted a new salary schedule based on four levels—bachelor's degree, master's degree, doctorate degree, and the mid-point between the master's and doctorate. Under the new salary schedule, the average annual faculty salary was $7,200 for a nine-month contract.

During 1963–64, the college's total operational budget was $1,087,118. The construction budget was $131,117.

College Division enrollment in fall 1962 equaled 1,250 students with a projected increase to 1,650 by fall 1964.

In a 1964 report to the board, Dr. Bergengren predicted that the College would reach its maximum enrollment by 1972. In preparation, he encouraged that immediate attention be given to planning for a second campus. He also noted the importance of considering instructional delivery methods such as television. Dr. Bergengren closed his speech with a profound statement that is still the guiding principle of Daytona Beach Community College to this day, "The college must never lose sight of the fact that it is a community centered institution, dedicated to the proposition that its only excuse for existence is wrapped up in the post high school needs of Volusia and Flagler Counties."

Early, undated photo showing a special evening class that trained hospitality workers in the latest billing and posting techniques. DBCC has always emphasized training for the hospitality industry. (Source: DBCC archives)

Above: Early, undated photo showing Lathe being unloaded for DBJC's mechanical lab. (Source: DBCC archives)

Left: Early 1960s photograph of President Bergengren (right) and Volusia County School Superintendent John Smiley (left) looking at the future DBJC Master Plan. (Source: DBCC archives)

DAYTONA BEACH JUNIOR COLLEGE

Volusia County Community College's first permanent home. The building was later converted to use by the Volusia County School Board as office space. (Source: DBCC archives)

Volusia County Community College's First Class

Volusia County Community College opened its doors on September 2, 1958, to 1,334 students. Fifty-three faculty members were employed to deliver instruction. Like Daytona Beach Junior College, VCCC opened in an array of temporary quarters. Of the 1,334 students and 53 faculty members, 188 transfer students and 13 faculty members were located in temporary quarters at 875 Second Avenue. The 198 vocational students, along with 11 faculty members, were located at Bethune-Cookman College's Trades Building. The remaining 1,018 adult students and 29 faculty members were located at a variety of sites around the county.

VCCC also formed a student government association. Officers included Leroy Brown, president; James Edwards, vice president; Johnnie Ruth Ellison, commissioner of rallies; Henry Floyd, commissioner of athletics; John Sharper, representative of sophomore class; Letty Ann Dowdell, treasurer; Ozell Williams, commissioner of social affairs; and Ralph Campbell, representative of men's senate.

From its inception in 1958 until its merger with Daytona Beach Junior College in 1965, VCCC served approximately 5,600 students in its various divisions.

Undated photo showing Volusia County Community College students working in the library prior to merger with Daytona Beach Junior College. (Source: DBCC archives)

Chapter 3

The Late 1960s

Changing Times, New Buildings, and a Merger

Above: Dr. Hollace E. Arment, chair of humanities and music, confers with Lorraine Cherico on a humanities project, December 1968. (Source: DBCC archives)

Right: Returning from Texas and celebrating DBJC's regional accreditation by the Southern Association of Colleges and Schools. (Left to right) Public Relations Director Bob Troup, President Roy Bergengren, WORD Radio staff reporter, College Dean R.W. Whetstone, and George Barton Sr. (Source: DBCC archives)

During the tumultuous 1960s, students were questioning values, forging their own identities, breaking with traditions, and protesting inequalities and injustices, even dress codes. Barriers were coming down.

Daytona Beach Junior College was a microcosm of the nation's college campuses. DBJC had graduated its first class and received regional accreditation and embarked on a path of growth and service to Volusia and Flagler Counties. In its immediate future was a merger with Volusia County Community College and the admission of its first black students. Several new buildings were constructed in the 1960s, and plans were laid for a second campus. Also in the 1960s, the College separated from the school system and created a District Board of Trustees for governance. Annual faculty evaluations were implemented, and the College abolished its dress code. The college president was even burned in effigy.

Published by—and for— Students of Daytona Beach Junior College, Florida

Merger with Volusia County Community College

As representative of the many barriers confronted by many organizations in the 1960s, Daytona Beach Community College and Volusia County Community College faced their own—the merger of the two institutions. The merger, although successful, was not completely smooth.

Many in the black community saw VCCC as more than an educational institution. It was also a community resource—one that led the way not only in providing a college education, but also in providing community leadership as well as cultural and athletic activities. The end for VCCC began with a communiqué from the Division of Community-Junior Colleges in May 1965. The communiqué stated:

We strongly recommend that each county operating two junior colleges immediately take some step toward consolidating these institutions. It appears likely that any delay on the part of counties moving toward full compliance may provide the basis for action on the part of the federal officials.

On May 11, 1965, the Volusia County Board of Public Instruction, the current governing unit for both Daytona Beach Community College and Volusia County Community College, voted to merge the two institutions. A plan was developed that would allow sophomore students at Volusia County Community College to complete their studies; however, new students for fall 1965 would be required to enroll at Daytona Beach Junior College.

The merger brought to a close the dynamic efforts being undertaken at Volusia County Community College. It also required a redistribution of staff. After the merger was completed, Mr. Greene, VCCC's president, was appointed as director of Guided Studies at Daytona Beach Junior College. Later, he was named dean of continuing education. He retired in 1973 and spent several years teaching English and education at Bethune-Cookman College. He died in 1987. Today, his memory lives on in the form of a Great Floridian plaque located at the J. Griffen Greene Student Resource Center, Building 300, on the Daytona Beach Campus of Daytona Beach Community College.

Many additional staff members from VCCC also joined DBJC, including Charles Mathis, mathematics instructor; Oliver L. Perkins, dean of instruction at VCCC; Julia Webb, director of guidance; Jacqueline D. Washington, guidance counselor; and Bernard Smith, dean of adult education.

One noted early faculty member at VCCC was Yvonne S. Golden, a teacher of health and physical education. After a successful career as an educator and principal in California, Ms. Golden was elected in 2003 as mayor of the city of Daytona Beach. She was re-elected in 2005. Unfortunately, Ms. Golden died in December 2006, in the middle of her second term as mayor.

The merger of the two institutions, while necessary for complying with the law and the long-term progress of the area, was bittersweet for many of the faculty, staff, and students of VCCC, as well as for the Daytona Beach community.

Of the three governing and advisory groups involved, the Board of Public Instruction of Volusia County, the governing board, and the Advisory Committee of Daytona Beach Junior College supported an immediate merger. The Volusia County Community College Advisory Committee supported merging the two institutions but recommended a more gradual approach involving additional study and a complete and gradual integration of the entire Volusia County School System. Several recommendations were presented by the VCCC president and advisory board for consideration.

The Board of Public Instruction did not consider the recommendations presented by VCCC and instead voted to immediately merge the two institutions. Following the successful vote, John H. Smiley, superintendent of schools, transmitted the following certificate to the State Board of Education in Tallahassee:

Certificate

I, **JOHN H. SMILEY,** *Secretary of the Board of Public Instruction of Volusia County, Florida, and Superintendent of Public Instruction of Volusia County, Florida do hereby certify that the foregoing Resolution entitled,*

"A RESOLUTION TO CONSOLIDATE THE VOLUSIA COUNTY COMMUNITY COLLEGE AND THE DAYTONA BEACH JUNIOR COLLEGE AND PROVIDING FOR AN EFFECTIVE DATE,"

was presented, considered, passed and adopted at a duly assembled meeting of the Board of Public Instruction of Volusia County, Florida held on the 11th day of May, A.D. 1965, in DeLand, Volusia County, Florida, and I further certify that the foregoing Resolution is a true and correct copy of the original Resolution duly adopted and spread upon the official minutes of said Board.

IN TESTIMONY WHEREOF, *I have hereunto set my hand and official seal this 11th day of May, A.D. 1965.*
/s/ John H. Smiley

Secretary to the Board of Public Instruction of Volusia County, Florida

Since VCCC was to remain open for one year in order to allow rising sophomore students the opportunity to graduate, President Greene was named vice president of what was then called the Volusia Center for the 1965–66 academic year. Former President Greene was then assigned to DBJC as director of guided studies and, finally, as dean of continuing education.

There were 517 college students at VCCC in 1964–65; however, there were a total of only 150 black students at DBJC and the Volusia Center in 1965–66. Sixteen of the full-time black faculty members were transferred to DBJC, with the remainder offered jobs the Volusia County K–12 system.

As DBJC completed its first decade of service in 1968, the implementation of four major recommendations set the stage for explosive growth over the following decades. The Governor's Commission on Quality Education recommended separation of junior colleges from county boards of education and making the up-to-then advisory boards the legal governing boards, concrete assurance of junior college graduates' acceptance at four-year institutions, increment of faculty salaries and faculty development (e.g., sabbaticals), and funds for building construction. These recommendations reflected then Governor Reubin Askew's commitment to education for all. His commitment is illustrated in the following quote:

For too long in too many cases, the college degree has been available on the basis of wealth, heredity, or place of residence as much as on interest and ability. We've had educational malnutrition among some of the brightest and most capable of our young citizens. No one should be locked into a cycle of poverty and ignorance, or even of near poverty and under education. . . It's not healthy for the person, for the community, or for democracy.

On July 1, 1968, the District Board of Trustees became the single administrative unit governing Daytona Beach Junior College. Dr. Bergengren, DBJC's president, told the new District Board of Trustees, "This is an historic occasion." He noted that the change in governing structure also coincided with the start of the college's second decade of operation. Paul Baker of Daytona Beach was elected chairman of the new board, and Morgan Welch of DeLand was elected vice chairman. The first action of the board was to reappoint Dr. Bergengren as president.

As DBJC completed its first decade of operation, Mr. Carl Shafer, registrar, announced that 82,411 students had attended the three college divisions—8,709 college credit; 21,612 vocational; 52,090 adult education.

Chapter 4

Coming of Age

The 1970s and '80s

Joseph "Joe" C. Petrock (center), as a student and star baseball player, poses with 1971 Miss DBCC Stacy Evens (left) and baseball team mascot Judy Mize (right). Petrock graduated from DBCC and became a member and chair of the Board of Trustees. (Source: DBCC archives)

Dave Marsh, DBCC alumnus and meteorologist with WESH-TV (an NBC affiliate), with Sharon Crow, director of alumni affairs. Crow is currently vice president of governmental relations for the College. (Source: DBCC archives)

Above: The National Swimming Championship team, April 1981. (Source: DBCC archives)

Left: DBCC's community choir, 1984. (Source: DBCC archives)

Aerial photograph of the Daytona Beach campus during the 1979–80 school year. Municipal Stadium is in the background. (Source: DBCC archives)

Nella and Morris Kelly display his Outstanding Alumnus Award at the 1975
Alumni Banquet. (Source: DBCC archives)

Presidential candidate Jimmy Carter (left) visits while on the campaign trail. Carter was
elected U.S. President in 1977, served one term, and was a Nobel Peace laureate in
1982. Others shown (left to right) Democratic party fund raiser and Volusia County
attorney Bill Crotty, Chair of DBCC Board of Trustees Henry Coleman, and President Polk
(back to camera). (Source: DBCC archives)

Above: Family members congratulate recent graduate Eddie Sullivan, May 1972. (Source: DBCC archives)

Left: David Lee Davis (left) receives 1987 Outstanding Alumni Award from Edwin Peck Jr., DBCC alumni chair. (Source: DBCC archives)

QUANTA class, 1984. QUANTA is a nationally recognized learning community where students and faculty work together to share their learning experiences. QUANTA integrates traditional college courses with a common theme and offers students the challenge of seeing and exploring the relationships between subjects and ideas within these subjects. (Source: DBCC archives and catalog)

Aerial photograph of the Daytona Beach Campus in the early 1970s. The newest building, the Bergengren Administration Building, is in the center. (Source: DBCC archives)

Aerial photo of the Daytona Campus taken during the 1979–80 academic year.
(Source: DBCC archives)

Above: Dedication of the Allied Health and Science Building, May 1982. (Left to right) Dr. Robert Fox, trustee; Larry Kelly, Daytona Beach mayor; Representative Tom Brown (behind Mr. Kelly); Dr. Charles Polk, president; Dr. T. K. Wetherell, vice president and state representative; Merhl Shoemaker, trustee; Senator Ed Dunn; and Leonard Sacks, trustee. (Source: DBCC archives)

Left: Artist rendition of the Allied Health and Science Building, which opened in 1982. The building provided state-of-the-art laboratories for training nurses and allied health professionals. It contained simulated hospital suites and two state-of-the-art operating rooms. (Source: DBCC archives)

The 1970s and '80s saw explosive growth as Daytona Beach Junior College came of age as the fastest growing community college in the state. Enrollment was outpacing classrooms. Students were flocking to DBJC for its academic and technical programs; innovative approach to education, job placement, and transfer rates; and its location. It was also time for a name change. In 1971, Daytona Beach Junior College became Daytona Beach Community College (DBCC). An entrepreneurial spirit permeated the college's vision as the youngest community college president in the country took charge.

On March 11, 1974, a memorandum from the Florida Department of Education confirmed Dr. Charles Henry Polk's appointment as the college's third regular president. Dr. Polk came to the college after serving as dean of the downtown campus of Florida Junior College at Jacksonville. At thirty-one years of age, Dr. Polk was not only the youngest president at DBCC when he took office, but he was also the nation's youngest college president. His background included bachelor's and master's degrees in sociology/psychology and an educational doctorate in adult education/community college. He assumed the office of the president in June 1974 and served until June 1990.

As a leader, Dr. Polk was bold and brash in his efforts to continue the development of the college. His progressive trustees, creative faculty and staff, and powerful legislative allies shared his vision; and together they shaped, molded, and defined DBCC as an incubator for innovative programs that educated the mind, enriched the spirit, and enlightened the soul.

The aggressive focus on growth, however, did not come without growing pains. On August 29, 1975, the local section of the *Daytona Beach Morning Journal* blazed, "DBCC May Close Doors to New Students in Spring." The accompanying article cited President Charles Polk as indicating that tight finances and burgeoning enrollments might lead to the college abandoning its "open door" policy. The problem was a result of funding and enrollment caps set by the state's Division of Community Colleges. DBCC's enrollment cap was set at 5,901 full-time equivalent students (FTEs). Appropriations statewide were approximately $155 million—representing a $30 million cut from the requests submitted by the colleges.

President Polk, noting that the College was mandated by the legislature to run twelve months, sought to limit fall enrollment, which had risen by 9 percent, to approximately 50 percent of the enrollment cap in order to ensure that the college would be able to operate for the entire year. Agonizing over turning away students, Polk said, "I don't want turning away students to become commonplace, but we may have to get used to it. In the spring semester, we probably won't accept any new students who would cut into the FTE. I think we can balance it that way." Board of Trustee's Chairman Henry Coleman concurred with Polk. He blamed the sagging economy for both a lack of funds at the state level and the enrollment boom at the local level, as people returned to school for retraining in an effort to land a job.

Dr. Charles Polk, DBJC's third president, presides at graduation. Director of Student Activities Sylvester Covington in background. (Source: DBCC archives)

President Polk with two original faculty members, Dan Stout and Mary Connelly, 1984. (Source: DBCC archives)

Light Years Ahead—The Advent of Technology

By the late 1970s, DBCC had created a learning environment that used the most advanced technology to support and enhance fundamental education. Relationships with businesses, industry, and other educational institutions were well established. A comprehensive core curriculum that provided the fundamentals for both college transfer and technical students was in place. In many ways, DBCC was light years ahead of its sister institutions, and students were reaping the benefits.

In August 1977, DBCC celebrated its first twenty years with this cake. The College had grown by leaps and bounds and was in the process of opening its first satellite campus in DeLand. Two other campuses (South and Flagler-Palm Coast) would follow in the next two years. Dr. Charles Polk was president. (Source: DBCC archives)

Jeanne Goddard, trustee (second from left), and former Governor LeRoy Collins (shaking Goddard's hand) talk at the College's twentieth anniversary in 1977. (Source: DBCC archives)

Benchmark Anniversary—Twenty Years and Growing

In 1977, Daytona Beach Community College celebrated its twentieth year of operation. Although still new by many standards, DBCC had rapidly matured into an institution that was making a significant difference in the lives of the citizens of Volusia and Flagler Counties. In addition to what was then referred to as the "main campus" in Daytona Beach, campuses, actually satellite centers, had been opened in West Volusia, South Volusia, and Flagler County.

The first of these satellite centers to open was the West Volusia Center, which began operation in August 1977. The center, located at 235 West New York Avenue, DeLand, in a former supermarket, immediately enrolled approximately three hundred students seeking college credit. The service area for the center was identified as DeLand and Deltona. Growth at this center was rapid, and in 1981, the Florida legislature appropriated $1 million toward a permanent site for the West Volusia area. The $1 million appropriation provided the "seed money" for what is now known as the DeLand campus, located at 1155 County Road.

The DeLand campus offers a wide range of associate of arts courses and some associate of science degree programs as well. The Bert Fish Building, built in 1995, houses advanced facilities for dental assisting, dental hygiene, nursing, science labs, and a multi-media learning center. The DeLand campus has continued to be the fastest growing campus, behind the Daytona Beach campus. The rapid growth led to the opening of the Deltona Center in 2004.

The College's second satellite center, the South Volusia Center, opened in August 1978 in the renovated second floor

The South Volusia Center began operation in August 1978. Located on the second floor of a strip mall on U.S. 1, the center enrolled 652 students in the first semester of operation. (Source: DBCC archives)

of a strip shopping mall in New Smyrna Beach. Initially, enrollment was 652 students. Enrollment at this center also grew rapidly, and by 1981, the college was holding classes at various other New Smyrna Beach locations, including Fish Memorial Hospital, New Smyrna Beach Senior High School, and Burns Elementary School in Oak Hill. The South Volusia Center, now called the New Smyrna Beach-Edgewater campus, is now located on its own site on Tenth Street in New Smyrna Beach.

The third satellite center, the Flagler-Palm Coast Center, was thirty-three miles north of the main campus in Daytona Beach. The center was opened in response to the rapid growth in Flagler County, due in part to the planned community of Palm Coast that was being built by the ITT Community Development Corporation. The center opened in space donated by ITT in fall 1979 with 360 students. Three years later, the Flagler-Palm Coast campus opened at its present site at 3000 Palm Coast Parkway Southeast.

The West Volusia Center began operation in August 1977. The center, located in an old supermarket building at 235 West New York Avenue, was slated to serve DeLand and Deltona. Three hundred students enrolled in the first semester of operation. (Source: DBCC archives)

August 1977, opening of the DeLand Center to serve West Volusia. (Left to right) Board Chair Jeanne Goddard, trustee George Williams (at the podium), President Charles Polk, State Representative Sam Bell, and State Representative Bill Conway. (Source: DBCC archives)

Dateline DBCC—Lights, Camera, Action

DBCC's connection with technology is almost as old as the college itself. The College's first major entry into the technology age was through television. From the first college-credit course it aired over Channel 2 to the latest high-tech, digital programming produced and aired over its own WCEU-TV, DBCC has understood the value of television in educating, enriching, and enlightening its community. Once again, DBCC took a simple medium and transformed it into one of the most powerful tools, and assets, in its educational repertoire.

As part of its normal development, DBCC developed and operated a media center. In keeping with the movement to offer educational opportunities via technology, DBCC, in the early 1980s, began to lease airtime from local television stations to broadcast college-credit courses. This arrangement worked well until the demand for airtime and DBCC's desire to produce and air creative programs about special events became so great that, according to Don Thigpen, someone told him, "You want so much airtime. Why don't you start your own station?"

On February 1, 1988, a new era began at DBCC when WCEU-TV took to the airwaves in Central Florida. WCEU's first general manager, Don Thigpen, recalls that deciding to take the step to open a television station was relatively easy, while actually carrying out the process proved to be quite a task. It took five years of planning and dealing with state and national politics before the television station became a reality. The station opened with three employees, all of whom had other duties. Initially, the station only broadcasted three hours daily for three days per week. Funding was extremely problematic until the station leased its transmitter on a rent-to-own basis. By January 1989, the station obtained certification from the Corporation for Public Broadcasting, giving it full recognition as a member of the Public Broadcasting Service.

Today the station is an integral part DBCC's educational program, serving both as a community service of the college and as a training laboratory for students in the Digital Television and Media Production Program.

Chapter 5

Winds of Change

Beyond Bricks and Mortar: The 1990s

The library in 1961. The building opened in 1960 as the Mary Karl Library. After extensive renovation and expansion, the building still serves as the library (Learning Resource Center) and also houses the Computing Commons. (Source: DBCC archives)

Left: Counselor and Associate Professor Larry Wesley delivers the keynote address at the Ninth Annual Minority Student Recruitment Day in April 1999. The event, since renamed the Annual Multicultural Recruitment Day, is designed to introduce students who may not have considered college as an option to the many services and programs offered by DBCC. (Source: DBCC archives)

Below: Students and teachers applaud during keynote address at the Ninth Annual Minority Student Recruitment Day in April 1999. Students from all high schools in Volusia and Flagler Counties are invited to attend the event. (Source: DBCC archives)

Faculty Award Recipients display their plaques, 1988–89. (Left to right) Professor of mathematics Dr. Thomas F. Davis—Student Advocacy; mathematics instructor Fred Ruby—Outstanding Adjunct Faculty; Associate Professor of history John Guthrie—Research and Professional Development; Records Supervisor Linda Lee—Instructional Support and Encouragement; and Professor of chemistry Jim Johnson—Teaching Excellence. (Source: DBCC archives)

Buildings on DBCC's Daytona Beach campus are brightly color coded and numbered, following the change from the original sequential numbering. One of the pitfalls of the sequential numbering system was that every building, including small service buildings, was included. Thus, small buildings that may have come and gone tended to leave "holes" in any attempt to chronologically describe DBCC's buildings. In addition, although buildings were initially numbered sequentially, they were built on various parts of the campus as the Campus Master Plan dictated. For example, Building 27 was a stone's throw from Building 15 but a cross-campus walk from Building 28. The systematic numbering and color-coding of buildings was a welcome change.

Some of DBCC's buildings, like those on many college campuses, were also named for individuals. Walk across campus, and hardly anyone asks where the Goddard Center, Lenholt Student Center, and Baker and Bailey Halls are. But these and others bear the names of ordinary people who played an extraordinary part in the college's birth and development. Beneath their public labels, the named buildings are dedicated to people who shared a vision, philosophy, and mission—making their dream of accessible education for all in their community a reality.

As mentioned earlier, Building 1 was built in 1959 as the original science building. A few years later, when the science department moved out of Building 1 and the Division of Communications moved in, the name was changed to the Herbert M. Davidson Communications Building. Davidson was an award-winning pioneer in the field of journalism, editor and publisher of the *Daytona Beach News-Journal*, and father of the University of Florida's School of Journalism.

Building 2 opened in 1960 as the Mary Karl Library. It was named after Mary Karl, who was instrumental in persuading Franklin Delano Roosevelt to turn the land, known then as the Welch Center and used as an army convalescent home and rehabilitation center, over to Volusia County for future use as a junior college. Building 2 has been renovated and enlarged three times and is now called the Learning Resource Center (Library) and also houses the Computing Commons.

Building 3 was the college's first administration building. On December 8, 1960, it was named Collins Hall after Governor LeRoy Collins, the Florida governor who was the political force behind the state's community college system. It originally housed administrative and faculty offices, the bookstore, and counseling.

Building 5, completed in 1963, was named the Bailey Hall of Technology after Thomas D. Bailey, state superintendent of schools when the Florida community college system was created. Bailey Hall originally housed the electronics, building construction, civil technology, and nursing programs; now Building 540, it houses Campus Safety and Facilities Planning on the first floor and the English Department on the second floor.

Building 7, the student center, was completed in 1966 and bears the name of Lillian Lenholt, a civic and community leader who championed the movement to have a community college in Volusia and Flagler Counties. She also served as the chair of the College's advisory committee. The Lenholt Student Center, Building 7, houses the cafeteria, student newspaper, and Student Government Association.

Other buildings bearing the names of DBCC's early supporters and shapers include Baker Hall, the Bergengren Building, and the Goddard Center for the Arts. Baker Hall opened in 1968. It was named for Paul Baker, a local labor leader and member of the original Daytona Beach Junior College Advisory Committee. That same year, the College gained its independence from the Volusia County School System, and Mr. Baker became the first chairman of the Board of Trustees. Baker Hall, Building 12, was the size of a football field and housed the printing, gas engines, refrigeration, photography, electronics, drafting, mill-working, dry-cleaning, and watch-repair programs. It has now been renovated, labeled Building 500, and houses the Mathematics Department and Academic Support Center.

Installation of Paul Baliker's Wellspring, a bronze manatee sculpture, which now keeps watch over the entrance to the Mary Karl Learning Resource Center (1994). Baliker taped a documentary, *For the Love of Manatee*, around creation of sculpture Wellspring. He has sculptures in many public places in the Daytona Beach area. His gallery is located in Palm Coast, Florida. (Source: DBCC archives)

Left: Collins Hall, the College's first administration building, opened in 1960. Pictured at the dedication (left to right) President Bergengren with Mary Collins and Governor LeRoy. (Source: DBCC archives)

Right: Bailey Hall opened in 1963 and housed most of the College's technology and occupational programs. (Source: DBCC archives)

Bottom: The Lenholt Student Center opened in 1966 to house the cafeteria, student activities and SGA offices, and the student newspaper, which it continues to house today. (Source: DBCC archives)

Groundbreaking for the Goddard Center, October 1977. Jeanne Goddard (center) with husband Dr. David Goddard (right) and daughter Susan (left). (Source: DBCC archives)

Building 16, now Building 110, was completed in 1972 and named after DBCC's president from 1960–74, Dr. Roy Bergengren. It served as the central administrative and continuing education offices until 1992 and now houses the Center for Business and Industry, Graphics Department, and the Florida Resource Center.

The Goddard Center for the Arts was named for Jeanne M. Goddard, an educational leader in Volusia County for more than forty years. She served on the Volusia County School Board as member and chair and the DBJC Advisory Committee. She became a charter member of the DBCC Board of Trustees and chaired it for eight years. She also served as senior vice president of the DBCC Foundation. The Goddard Center for the Arts contains vocal and drama performance and practice rooms as well as a black box theater.

Other named buildings include the Wetherell Student Services and Administration Building, the L. Gale Lemerand Center, and the William W. Schildecker Science Building on the Daytona campus, and the Bert Fish Building on the DeLand Campus. Named buildings under construction include the Mori Hosseini Hospitality Building and the Noah McKinnon Building on the Daytona campus.

The Wetherell Student Services and Administration Building, more commonly known as Building 100, was built to house administrative and student services in one location. The building is named after Tom Wetherell, father of T. K. Wetherell, former DBCC vice president, state representative, and current president of Florida State University.

Tom and T. K. Wetherell, DBCC vice president and state representative. Building 100 on the Daytona Campus is named the Wetherell Student Services and Administration Building. T. K. Wetherell is currently the president of Florida State University. (Source: DBCC archives)

Left: The Physical Education Building opened in 1962. It has been renovated and is now called the L. Gale Lemerand Center. (Source: DBCC archives)

Bottom: The L. Gale Lemerand Center, named after a former trustee and major donor. It houses a state-of-the-art fitness and aquatic center. (Source: DBCC archives)

The L. Gale Lemerand Building houses the College's gymnasium and aquatic center. The current building is a renovated structure that encompasses the College's original gymnasium, which opened in 1962 and was called the "Scots Palace," and the original outdoor swimming pool. Mr. Lemerand provided financial support for the building renovation and for health education and intercollegiate sports activities at DBCC. He owns Gale Industries, which started as an insulation sub-contracting firm in the Midwest. In 1995, he was named Florida Entrepreneur of the Year in the construction and real estate division. He has served on the DBCC Board of Trustees and on the WCEU Channel 15 board.

The William W. Schildecker Science Building. Located on the Daytona campus, this building houses all laboratory science courses. Named after Dr. William W. Schildecker, president of the Bert Fish Health Endowment Foundation, which has been a major benefactor to DBCC. (Source: DBCC archives)

The current Allied Health and Nursing Building was built to house both the health and science programs. With rapid growth in both areas, by the 1990s, there was a need for additional space. The solution was to build the William W. Schildecker Science Building to house the College's science programs.

The DeLand campus bears the distinction of being the only campus other than the Daytona campus to have named buildings. The Bert Fish Building on the DeLand campus houses the nursing, dental hygiene, and health science laboratory programs. The Bert Fish Health Endowment provided financial support for constructing the building, which was named in honor of Judge Bert Fish, founder of the endowment. The second named building on the DeLand campus is the Amory Underhill Child Care Center. Mr. Underhill is a former chairman of the Bert Fish Health Endowment.

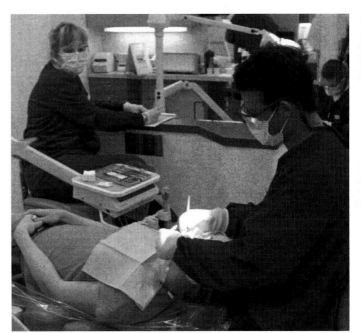

Beyond the Buildings

Change and transition were the watchwords of the '90s. An explosion in information and technology was powering a new world order. Higher education faced enormous challenges—balancing higher costs and fewer resources with the demands of rapidly changing student demographics, employer needs, and community expectations.

The president, who had sown the seeds of innovative programs, capital expansion, and academic excellence, was handing over the reins to a young, Kennedyesque community college product, Dr. Philip R. Day Jr. In addition to being a former community college student, Dr. Day had previous service as the president of Cape Cod Community College in Massachusetts and Dundalk Community College in Baltimore, Maryland. As he embarked on the job of

leading DBCC toward the new century, Dr. Day had unique ideas of what a community college, and specifically DBCC, should look like and how it should conduct business. The winds of change had swept into office a man who understood the dynamics of the marketplace, that education was a business, and that the product had to be students with skilled hands, sharp minds, and tolerant hearts.

An immediate task for Dr. Philip Day Jr.'s presidency upon his arrival in 1990 was preparation for DBCC's fourth reaffirmation of accreditation by the Southern Association of Colleges and Schools, Commission on Colleges. Under his leadership, the College underwent a carefully orchestrated "community listening process" designed to gather a clear understanding of the community's needs that could be delivered by DBCC. The community feedback was incorporated into the DBCC's Strategic Plan and the accreditation reaffirmation process.

Key terms, such as "high-tech" and "high touch" rapidly became shorthand phrases for a philosophy that permeated every facet of DBCC as the new president, his trustees, faculty, and staff strove to create a robust learning environment that was realistic, effective, responsible, visible, "plugged-in," and "user friendly."

Achieving new dimensions of academic excellence and student success was the clear goal. Engaging DBCC's constituent groups was vital. Doing more with less state funding was the looming obstacle.

It became clear from the community listening sessions that a college education was no longer just about job training or preparing students for advanced degrees. Students had to graduate with more than the fundamental knowledge and practical skills needed to navigate the highly technical world successfully. Employers wanted skilled workers who also could think, be responsible, respectful, compassionate, tolerant, and ethical. And if students missed these basic "dos and don'ts" along the way, then DBCC was expected to teach them—or so business, industry, civic, community, and religious leaders said during the college's listening sessions.

The traditional college classroom and lesson plan had to change. DBCC faculty had real world experience, so they knew they could teach students to balance drives and pressures for success in the workforce or college classroom with tolerance, responsibility, and respect for the ideas and value systems of others. The challenge was showing them why it mattered.

Health Education Goes High Tech

In early 1997, a new guy arrived on campus to sit in on respiratory therapy, nursing, and emergency medical classes. Named Stan, short for Standard Man, this guy is neither a student nor instructor. Stan is a technologically advanced training manikin capable of mimicking almost any disease, aliment, or physiological function. Imagine having a "patient" who goes into cardiac arrest upon command and allows students to practice cardiac resuscitation over and over to a mastery level. Stan is capable of responding to drugs and other interventions and take on the signs and symptoms of a range of conditions and diseases, all at the direction of the computer program selected by the instructor.

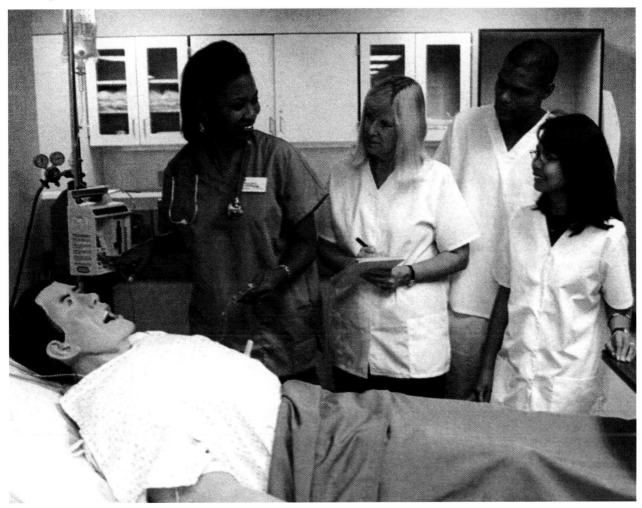

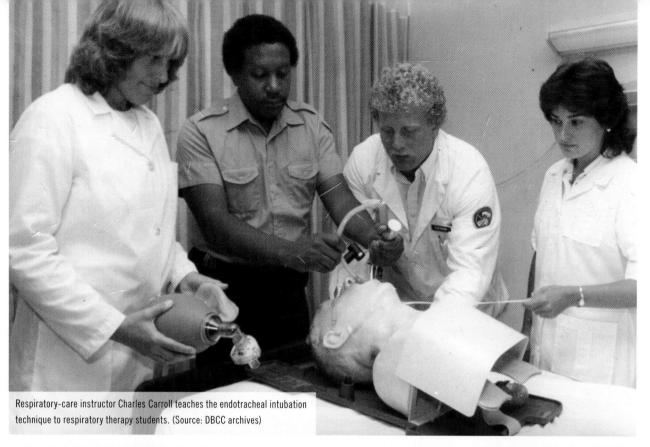

Respiratory-care instructor Charles Carroll teaches the endotracheal intubation technique to respiratory therapy students. (Source: DBCC archives)

Hugs and smiles mark the December 1990 nursing graduation ceremony.
(Source: DBCC archives)

Left: Dr. Paul Thompson, vice president, congratulates Lisa Voorhees at the 1990 Awards Convocation. Voorhees, a respiratory therapy student, received awards for Who's Who in American Community Colleges and the Blue Key Hall of Fame. (Source: DBCC archives)

Bottom: Spring 1993, Surgical Technology program display of surgical instruments at Volusia Mall amazes onlookers. The surgical technology program, one of the College's oldest allied health programs, supplies surgical technologists to all of the area hospitals' operating rooms. (Source: DBCC archives)

The Advanced Technology Center is Born

Also, in the fall of 1997, DBCC began a dialogue that led to a major partnership venture with Volusia and Flagler Counties to develop the Advanced Technology Center (ATC). The center, situated on one hundred acres of land on Williamson Blvd., opened in fall 2001. The opening class had 176 dual-enrolled high school students along with over 500 adult students. High school students were juniors or seniors who desired to earn credit, or in some cases, a full degree, toward one of the over thirty technical areas offered at the ATC. Opening of the ATC hailed the arrival of a new type of technology education for Volusia and Flagler Counties.

Although dual enrollment has been in existence for many years, the ATC provided the first opportunity for students to make significant progress toward a college-level technical degree or certificate while still earning credit toward high school graduation.

Chapter 6

Daytona Beach Community College

A Pictorial View

If a picture is worth a thousand words, the following pages are worth more than a million. Each picture will likely stimulate a unique memory for those who "remember when." For others, some of the pictures will fold back the pages of history and reveal what was. Finally, the pictures, some from the distant past and some from the recent past, tell another component of the story of Daytona Beach Community College as it was, as it was becoming, and as it is today. Enjoy!

Aerial view of the DBJC site showing army barracks and Highland
Presbyterian Church, October 1959. (Source: DBCC archives)

Students gather outside of the Issena Inn in the early days of DBJC. (Source: DBCC archives)

Campus scene on the Daytona campus after the completion of Building 1.
(Source: DBCC archives)

Above: Early, undated photograph of nursing class. (Source: DBCC archives)

Left: Groundbreaking for Baker Hall. (Left to right) John Smiley, Volusia County Schools superintendent; Paul Baker, DBJC Advisory Committee chair; Governor LeRoy Collins; and President Roy Bergengren. (Source: DBCC archives)

Scene from early typing class at Volusia County Community College prior to merger with DBCC. (Source: DBCC archives)

Above: Daytona campus scene in 1967 showing Buildings 1 and 2. (Source: DBCC archives)

Right: DBCC's celebration of its twentieth anniversary, 1977. (Left to right) Jeanne Goddard, chair of Board of Trustees, and trustees Leonard Sacks and Ray Mercer. (Source: DBCC archives)

The Heart Run, October 1981. (Source: DBCC archives)

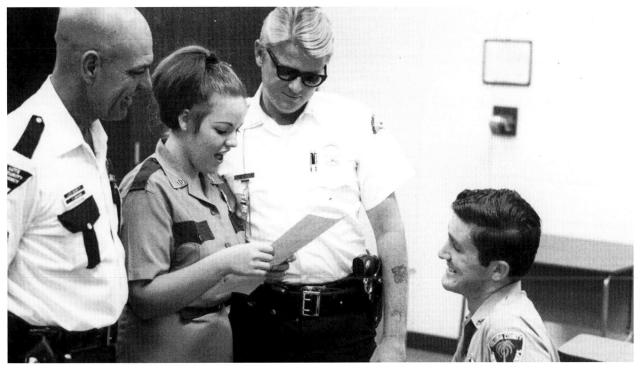

Early law criminal justice class. (Source: DBCC archives)

South campus dedication, 1988. (Left to right) DBCC trustees Kenneth
Hawthorne, David Burt, George Williams, Wayne Beighle, Sally Gillespie,
and President Charles H. Polk. (Source: DBCC archives)

West (DeLand) campus dedication, 1989. (Left to right) DBCC trustees
Kenneth Hawthorne, Wayne Beighle, George Williams, David Burt, and
President Charles H. Polk. (Source: DBCC archives)

DAYTONA BEACH COMMUNITY COLLEGE

February 1989

Journal

Rob Layman, marketing

South Campus serving students

The new South Campus, 940 10th St., New Smyrna, opened its doors to students on Jan. 5. Student enrollment stands at approximately 1,200, according to Kathy Miller, south campus director. The 18,444 square-foot building, designed by the Orlando-based architectural firm of Vickrey, Oversat, Awsumb & Associates, was completed at a cost of $1,640,974, according to John Justus, director of facilities planning.

Cover of Daytona Beach Community College's journal featuring the new south campus, 1989. (Source: DBCC archives)

New West (DeLand) campus sign. (Source: DBCC archives)

Current Administration Building on the DeLand campus. (Source: DBCC archives)

Lobby of the Advanced Technology College Center. Classes are offered at the center for dual-enrolled high school students and adult college students. (Source: DBCC archives)

Advanced Technology College Center on Williamson Blvd. (Source: DBCC archives)

Computing Commons on Daytona campus. (Source: DBCC archives)

Academic Support Center on Daytona campus. (Source DBCC archives)

Top: Original Deltona Center in rented space, opened August 1980. (Source: DBCC archives)

Right: Newest building at the Deltona Center. (Source: DBCC archives)

Top: Administrative Building at Flagler-Palm Coast campus. (Source: DBCC archives)

Right: Former Representative Shirley Chisholm prepared to deliver commencement speech. (Source: DBCC archives)

Then—April 1966, sophomore Wendy Ragsdale writes for the *Bagpiper* student newspaper on a manual typewriter. (Source: DBCC archives)

Now—2005, Associate Professor Roger Rowan (left) works with students in automated machine shop at the Advanced Technology College campus. (Source: DBCC archives)

Now—Spring 2007, students use computers for word processing and class tutorials. (Source: DBCC archives)

Then—1960s, small-motors instructors display various learning
aids and a recording machine. (Source: DBCC archives)

Left: Representative Samuel Bell participates in the 1978–79 Dollars for Scholars Campaign. (Source: DBCC archives)

Bottom: President Philip Day Jr. (1990–98) confers with Professors Richard Zelley and Cynthia Avens on QUANTA program.

Faculty march to Annual Awards Convocation in early 1980s. (Source: DBCC archives)

Chapter 7

Stepping Into the Future

Milestones and Indicators of Excellence

A view from the first floor of the Student Services and Administration Building showing the Madrigal Singers performing a Christmas concert with some of the more than fifty foreign flags in the background representing the many countries from which DBCC's student body hails. (Source: DBCC archives)

Information Center

Top: After humble beginnings in cramped quarters in the library, WCEU, DBCC PBS-15 now occupies a modern studio (Center for Telecommunications) on the northwest corner of the Daytona campus. The station delivers a wide range of educational programs, services, and information to Central Florida homes. (Source: DBCC archives)

Right: The pool inside the Lemerand Center. (Source: DBCC archives)

Top: National Junior College Athletic Association Fastpitch Region VIII—Florida state champions, 1995. Gaye Lynn Wilson, head coach; Chuck Baylor, assistant coach; Tom Marsh, assistant coach. Players—Tami Arnold, Janet Brown, Amy Gregory, Vanessa Herberger, Katie Hill, Heather Hold, Dawn Jackson, Heather Jones, Karen Jose, Jennifer Kintz, Stacey Kirk, Victoria Lanier, Meredith Monte, Misty Moore, Danielle Mortiere, Megan Shryock, Ali Sieracki, and Lisa Wyatt. (Source: DBCC archives)

Left: Students hurrying to class pass the Lemerand Center on the Daytona campus. The Allied Health and Nursing Building is in the background. (Source: DBCC archives)

Below: President Kent Sharples (left), assisted by Board of Trustees Chairman Mr. James Gardner (right), confers an honorary associate of arts degree on L. Gale Lemerand, vice chairman of the Board of Trustees.

From its humble beginnings, providing access and the pursuit of excellence was always the driving force for DBCC. Over the years, in addition to establishing itself as an institution of academic excellence, a leader in innovative education, and a pacesetter for its contribution to economic development, DBCC has also impacted the social and cultural development of the citizens of Volusia and Flagler Counties.

DBCC's international reputation for the visual arts is anchored in its photography program. No other two-year program could draw names like Mary Ellen Mark, Eddie Adams, Gordon Parks, and others as lecturers. But like a panoramic option on a camera, the program expanded into a high-tech field of film, video, digital, and graphic arts. And the small professional exhibits that once took center stage in the Goddard Center found a permanent home in the stunning Southeast Center for Photographic Studies, the only photography museum in the nation affiliated with a community college.

DBCC visual arts students have incredible resources available that few of their peers can only imagine. At the same time, the program encourages students and faculty to live the college mission of teaching, learning, and community service. Following the 9/11 tragedy at the New York Twin Towers, DBCC's Southeast Museum of Photography was one of few museums in the country to host a traveling display of photographs depicting the tremendous destruction and despair. Thousands of patrons visited the museum to view this display.

Not Just Another Trade School

DBCC's roots lie in the Mary Karl Vocational School, originally funded through the Smith-Hughes Act. The premise was simple—train students to get jobs. Students learned everything from watch repair to dry cleaning, mill working to sewing-machine operation. Hundreds were trained as war-production workers during World War II. But as the economy shifted

A view of the first and second floors of the Southeast Museum of Photography. (Source: DBCC archives)

from industrial to knowledge-based and technology shifted from machines to computers, employers demanded skilled workers, specialized training, and a rapid response to their workforce needs. They depended upon DBCC to provide that highly trained, technically skilled, readily available pool. As discussed earlier, DBCC, while embracing trade and industrial training, quickly became an incubator for innovative programs, advanced technology, and dynamic partnerships.

Today, DBCC offers more than one hundred technical, career, and professional preparatory programs. In addition to the School of Arts and Sciences, which focuses on preparing students for transfer and supporting the technical, career, and professional preparatory programs with general education courses, there are three other schools of the college with specific training and career preparatory focuses.

First, the School of Health, Human, and Public Services provides training and career preparation to nurses, allied health practitioners, human services workers, and fire, police, and related public-service workers.

Second, the School of Business and Library Services provides training and career preparation for legal assistants, entry-level accounting positions, and a wide range of office and administrative services. Hospitality and culinary career preparation are also mainstays of the school. Library services are also organizationally administered through the school.

Third, the School of Technology and Occupational Programs offers a full range of computer and Internet career programs along with electronics and engineering related programs. Recently, this school introduced a simulations and robotic program.

Chapter 8

A New Century

Banner in front of Building 150 touting DBCC's new status as a baccalaureate degree-granting institution. The College was approved by the State Board of Education to offer the bachelor of applied science degree in supervision and management in April 2005. The Southern Association of Colleges and Schools, Commission on Colleges approved DBCC's application to move from Level I to Level II in December 2005, clearing the way for the implementation of the new four-year degree program. (Source: DBCC archives)

Above: Dr. Kent Sharples (right) and host Clark Maxwell (left) interview Dominican Republic President Leonel Fernandez (center) during an Eyes on Education taping on DBCC's PBS Channel 15. Almost fifty years after its own birth, DBCC has entered into a partnership with the Dominican Republic to assist in developing a community-college system in this rapidly developing Caribbean nation. (Source: DBCC archives)

Right: Dr. Kent Sharples confers with then Governor Jeb Bush at commencement in May 2006. Bush delivered the commencement address to a full house at the Daytona Beach Ocean Center. (Source: DBCC archives)

Miss America 2004 displays her crown to clients and staff at the Women's Center. (Source: DBCC archives. Used with permission.)

Dr. Kent Sharples (left) and Dr. Oswald Bronson (right), then president of Bethune-Cookman College (now Bethune-Cookman University), pose with Ericka Dunlap, Miss America 2004, after she toured DBCC's Women's Center. The Women's Center provides support and guidance to women who seek to change their lives by re-entering the job market or furthering their education. (Source: DBCC archives. Used with permission of Miss America Corporation.)

Dr. Kent Sharples and Board of Trustees Chairman Joe Petrock confer an honorary Associate of Science degree on Governor Jeb Bush after he delivered the 2006 commencement address. (Source: DBCC archives)

Graduates celebrate after commencement address by Governor Jeb Bush, 2006. The College awarded over 3,500 degrees, certificates, and diplomas during the 2005–06 academic year. (Source. DBCC archives)

Groundbreaking ceremony for the Mori Hosseini Center. (Left to right) Joe Petrock, chair, Board of Trustees; Dr. Mary Bennett, trustee; Forough B. Hosseini, trustee; Greg Smith (background), trustee; Mori Hosseini; Dr. Kent Sharples, president; and Bill Davison, trustee. (Source: DBCC archives)

Dr. Belle Wheelan, president of the Southern Association of Colleges and Schools, poses with college officials prior to delivering the May 2007 commencement address. Dr. Wheelan is the first female, the first former community college president, and first black person to lead the association, which is responsible for accrediting all institutions of higher education in the eleven southern states. (Source: Bob Knight Photography. Used with permission.)

Ladies' Golf Team after winning the National Junior College Athletic Association Championship in 2003. (Front row, left to right) Aubrey McCormick, Julie Best, and Brenda McLarnon. (Back row, left to right) Ulnka Ljungman, Laura Brown (coach), and Jessica Trein. (Source: DBCC archives)

Ladies' Golf Team after winning the National Junior College Athletic Association Championship in 2004. (Left to right) Kaci Howington, Laura Brown (coach), Jessica Trein, Kayla Shaul, Kristy McLaughlin, and Ashley Janzen. (Source: DBCC archives)

Above: Ladies' Golf Team after winning the 2005 National Junior College Athletic Association Championship. (Left to right) Jess Mullane, Deah Ruebel, Laura Brown (coach), Sara Hutchins, Kristy McLaughlin, Kayla Shaul, Christina VanWart, and Ashley Janzen. (Source: DBCC archives)

Left: Frank Lombardo, academic vice president, presents the Faculty Advocacy Award to Professor Mercedes Clement, Faculty Senate president for 2005–06. (Source: DBCC archives)

Below: First graduates of the College's Executive Leadership Development program, November 2002. The program, started by President Kent Sharples after his arrival in 1999, evolved into the Leadership Development Institute, which provides continuous career development activities for the College's employees. (Front row, left to right) Joanne Pinkston-McDuffie, Nancy Morgan, Sue Hawkins, and Charlene Latimer. (Middle row, left to right) Dr. Doug Peterson, Kristy Presswood, Laura Phillips, Sandra Sessions-Robertson, Sandra Offiah, Laurie van Dusen, Dora Moses, Dr. Michael Vitale, and Joseph Roof. (Back row, left to right) President Sharples; Dr. Dale Campbell, professor and University of Florida program director; Vickie Melton; Margaret Overbey; Roberto Lombardo; Dr. Charles Carroll, vice president and program coordinator; Fred Fathi. (Source: DBCC archives)

Executive Director Bruce Dunn of WCEU, PBS Channel 15, confers with Ned Harper, director of Small Business Development Center (SBDC), at the 2006 Fall Festival of Grants. The television station and the SBDC depend heavily on grants for operational funding. The College receives over $7 million annually in grant funding to supplement its budget and to offer innovative services to students and the community. Dr. Nancy Morgan, associate vice president for Resource Development and Planning, manages the grants procurement process. (Source: DBCC archives)

Dr. Donald Matthews, director of International Affairs, points to the international display at the 2006 Fall Festival of Grants. The International Affairs Department has assisted with bringing international students from more than fifty countries to study at DBCC. The department depends heavily on grants and receives approximately $350,000 annually in grant funding. (Source: DBCC archives)

Above: Associate Professor of Computer Science Jameal Adkins reviews the Bridge Research Program display at the 2006 Fall Festival of Grants. The Bridge Research Program receives grant funding in excess of $200,000 annually. The focus of the grant is to produce more PhDs in the medical and biomedical sciences among minority students. Dr. Ram Nayar, professor of microbiology, is the program director. (Source: DBCC archives)

Left: Vice President for Economic Development Robert Williams confers with Dean Stanley Sidor at the 2006 Fall Festival of Grants on the iTec grant. This $4.5 million grant focused on ensuring that the Central Florida faculty who teach computer science were trained on the most advanced equipment available. (Source: DBCC archives)

Dr. Sharples (right) confers with representatives from the Wuxi Institute of Technology from China. Representatives from the institute, founded in 1959, have visited DBCC on several occasions to study DBCC's approach to delivering education. (Source: DBCC archives)

Above: Students from Ireland celebrate after studying digital media and working at Channel 15 for ten weeks. In additional to the technical skills, the students are also engaged in cross-cultural learning. Half of the students are Protestant from Northern Ireland, and the other half are Catholic from the Republic of Ireland. (Source: DBCC archives)

Right: President Kent Sharples and his wife Linda with Bill Olivari at the 2007 commencement ceremony. Olivari is the president of the College's Foundation. The Foundation is a direct support organization of the College that raises funds for scholarships, building projects, laboratory equipment, and other college needs. (Source: Bob Knight Photography. Used with permission.)

President Sharples, at the May 2007 commencement, displays the first bachelor of applied science degree to be awarded by the College. The College received approval from the Florida Board of Education to award the bachelor degree in April 2005. Accreditation for the degree was granted by the Southern Association of Colleges and Schools in December 2005. Twelve students were in the first graduating class. (Source: Bob Knight Photography. Used with permission.)

The first bachelor of applied science in supervision and management class. (Left to right) Dr. Eileen Hamby, vice president of baccalaureate programs; students Gary Vela, Tiemey Roland, Fleurette Clement, Amy Acker, Josh Casey, Lloyd Parrish, Margarita Sullivan, Dipti Rodriguez, Haywood Peterson, Amy Wolf, Tiffany Phillips, Grace Termer, and Soli Reynolds; and Frank Lombardo, vice president for academic affairs. (Graduates not pictured: Eric Carlson, Sylvia Christiansen, and Terri Hannah) (Source: DBCC archives)

Daytona Beach Community College approached the new century with a new president, Dr. D. Kent Sharples. The tall man, with a soft drawl and quick smile, spoke of fostering a college spirit of teaching, learning, and community service. He promised an institution that would reach out to the community through partnerships and projects. He saw the need to expand DBCC's role and involvement in programs and services that would benefit its students, faculty, and community.

After assuming the presidency in July 1999, Dr. Sharples, like his predecessors, was determined to continue to move DBCC to the highest possible level of performance. Among his many accomplishments were the implementation of the Leadership Development Institute, Succession Planning, and an award-winning Planning and Participatory Governance process. Probably the most significant event of Dr. Sharples's presidency occurred on April 19, 2005, when the Florida State Board of Education unanimously approved DBCC's application to offer a baccalaureate degree. The degree, the Bachelor of Applied Science in Supervision and Management, is designed to provide the next level of education to associate of science graduates. The regional accrediting agency, the Southern Association of Colleges and Schools, Commission on Colleges, approved DBCC's application for moving from Level I (associate degree) to Level II (bachelor's degree) in December 2005, offically making the College a four-year institution.

As DBCC begins its fiftieth-anniversary celebration, an agreement to bring medical education to the area has been completed. Florida State University, which opened its College of Medicine in June 2000, has selected Daytona Beach Community College as the location for one of its community-based sites. The arrangement will place DBCC in the role of being host to approximately forty students in their third and fourth years of medical school.

The University of Central Florida (UCF) has always been DBCC's primary partner for upper division education. UCF has had a physical presence on the Daytona campus for well over a decade. In an effort to bring additional educational opportunities to the area, DBCC established the University Center in 2005. The mission of the University Center is to collaborate with other colleges and universities to offer upper-division and graduate study and degrees to the citizens of Volusia and Flagler Counties. Currently, nine schools are affiliated with DBCC's University Center.

Online Education Becomes Virtual

In July 2003, just a few years short of the fiftieth anniversary of the DBCC's "physical birth," DBCC's Virtual College was born. The College had experimented with various instructional delivery methods, including television courses and instructional technology. Classes were broadcast from campus to campus through an interactive television system designed specifically for instructional purposes, and some courses were offered on-line via computers. These methods had met with success, but it was now time for the college to dedicate a systematic approach to on-line education. The Virtual College was charged with carrying out this task.

The on-line course initiative was approached with the same level of planning and rigor that DBCC puts into the development of all of its programs. Research into the best practices was conducted, and a plan was developed. Of particular concern was the challenge of ensuring that on-line instruction met the same rigor and quality as face-to-face instruction. To meet this challenge, delivery and teaching standards were developed, and a quality control system was implemented.

Today, DBCC offers a broad range of options for on-line instructions, ranging from classes taught entirely on-line to classes taught 25 to 75 percent on-line. Students can earn all required general education credits on-line as well as earn entire associate of arts and associate of business degrees on-line. Approximately four thousand students are currently enrolled in on-line courses. On-going assessments indicate that the learning outcomes for on-line students are equivalent to that for face-to-face students.

Intellectual Capital

The value of any item can be appraised in terms of its tangible and intangible qualities, direct and indirect benefits, and presence and absence in the lives of those it touches. DBCC, as any educational body, is no different.

Educators and business leaders state that "intellectual capital" is a key indicator in a community's economic health. That means communities will become poorer if the minds of citizens are not educated and if there is a failure to provide a sufficient pool of well-paying, skilled jobs. College graduates and highly skilled workers will leave for areas that offer more economic opportunities.

DBCC has always been in the midst of the economic and social fabric of the area as an asset tapped as needed. Perhaps the real value of DBCC can be best assessed by looking at life in the area if DBCC hadn't been here.

Life without DBCC? It's hard to imagine.

Chapter 9

The Evolution Continues

There is no ending to this book, only thoughts on how far DBCC has come, future plans, and its relevance in the lives of those it has touched. Practically everyone in the Volusia and Flagler County areas, and many beyond, has been impacted by DBCC. The majority of professional and technical workers in the area received training at DBCC.

The list is so long that it would take an entire book to begin to paint a full and accurate picture. A quick way to gauge DBCC's impact would be to take a look around at the area workers. Whether it is health care, public service, or private business, the odds are very high that the skill-workers received part or all of their education and training at DBCC. Daytona Beach Community College's presence has indeed played a major role in shaping the present of our service area and will continue to do so in the future. Just as the visionaries who were responsible for laying the foundation for what DBCC is today, the future depends on similar actions from those who now stand on the foundation that DBCC has created.

In the spirit of continuing evolution, the Board of Trustees voted in September 2007 to change the College's name from "Daytona Beach Community College" to "Daytona Beach College." This change emphasizes our intent to continue serving the community. Adding selected baccalaureate education illustrates the College's response to that intent. The change in no way diminishes the College's role in serving the community; in fact, adding baccalaureate education serves the community in the same spirit that DBJC and VCCC set out in to serve the community in 1958.

Photograph of Will Harry Patrinelli graduating from DBCC's adult high school at age ninety. His goal was to become a realtor. (Source: DBCC archives)

Dr. Kent Sharples, DBCC's current president, reflects and looks to the future. (Source: DBCC archives)

President Sharples, Board Chair Joe Petrock, and Glyn Johnston consult
on College plans. (Source: DBCC archives)

Appendix

Daytona Beach Community College's Presidents

DBCC has had five permanent and two interim presidents during its fifty years of operation. Each president brought a unique vision and served to move the College to the next level dictated by the current challenges. Collectively, but in their own individual ways, they provided the guiding hands that shaped DBCC into the excellent institution that it is today.

Name	Dates of Service
Dr. James M. Snyder	January 1, 1958–June 30, 1960
Dr. N. B. McMillian (interim)*	July 1960–August 1960
Dr. Roy F. Bergengren	August 1960–May 1974
Dr. Charles H. Polk	June 1974–April 1990
Dr. Philip R. Day Jr.	April 1990–August 1998
Dr. H. Hartsell (interim)**	August 1998–June 1999
Dr. D. Kent Sharples	July 1999–Present

* Dr. McMillian was one of the college's first employees and was serving as dean of the Transfer Division when he was tapped to serve as interim president upon Dr. Synder's departure.

** Dr. Hartsell previously served as president of Pensacola Junior College. After his retirement, he served for almost one year at DBCC following Dr. Day's tenure.

Daytona Beach Community College's Board of Trustees

Members of the District Board of Trustees are appointed by the governor. The positions are voluntary in nature; however, the responsibility is tremendous. Along with many other duties and legal responsibilities, the board is responsible for hiring and supervising the president and establishing policies for the institutions.

The College was initially operated under the authority of the Volusia County School Board with the DBJC Advisory Committee serving as the link between the school board and the college administration. The board was formally reorganized into the District Board of Trustees, officially dropping the designation DBJC Advisory Committee in July 1968. Paul Baker was elected to serve as the first board chairman. The new board assumed the full policy-making responsibility, which was formerly held by the Volusia County School Board.

Baker, Paul

Beighle, Wayne J.

Bennett, Mary

Blossom, Roland J.

Brown, Sarah E.

Burden, Beatriz H.

Burt, David

Callender, Lynnette J.

Clegg, John

Coleman, Henry, Jr.

Creal, Charles

Davidson, Herbert M.

Davison, William H.

Desai, Pramila S.

Ford, James

Fox, Robert G.

Gardner, James

Gautier, E. William

Gillespie, Sally I.

Goddard, Jeanne M.

Graham, John

Harvey, Ellery H.

Hawthorne, Kenneth B.

Hosseini, Forough B.

Korwek, Alexander D.

Lacy, Ben W., Jr.

Lemerand, L. Gale

Lenssen, William

Leonard, Albert J., III

Lichtigman, Charles S.

Likes, Christopher K.

Mallory, Peter E.

Martin, Catheryn S.

McKenney, John G., Jr.

McKinnon, Noah, Jr., Esq.

Megonegal, E. Russell

Mercer, Ray L.

Paul, Mary Ann

Petrock, Joseph C.

Primus, Bobbie J.

Roser, Richard

Sacks, Leonard M.

Sander, Theodor J.

Schildecker, William W.

Scullion, William

Shoemaker, Merhl E.

Smolen, Alan

Starke, L. C.

Smith, Gregory

Wadsworth, L. E.

Wadsworth, Wilhelmina

Welch, Morgan

Williams, George R.

DBCC's Buildings and Names

Building Name/Old Number/Current Number	Source of Name
Language Building/1/340 The College's first building.	Never formally named
Mary Karl Learning Resource Center/2/210	Mary Brennan Karl
Collins Hall/3/120	Former Governor LeRoy Collins
L. Gale Lemerand Center/Fitness and Aquatic Center/4/310	Former Board of Trustee member
Bailey Hall/5/540—Houses campus safety and faculty offices.	Former State Superintendent of Instruction Thomas Bailey
Lenholt Student Center/7/130—Houses cafeteria and student activities office.	Mrs. Eric Lenholt, charter member and chairman of the College's Advisory Committee
Humanities/Auditorium/8/220	Never formally named
Originally built as the Automotive Building. Renovated for Cosmetology/10/510	Never formally named
Academic Support Center/Math/12/500 (Most of Building 12 was demolished. Building 500, a new building, is attached to a portion of old Building 12.)	Building 12 was named Baker Hall for Paul Baker, a local labor leader and member of the original DBJC Advisory Committee.

DBJC's First Yearbook

InnKeeper—1959

The first yearbook, ninety-two pages (Courtesy of Skip Lowery)

Foreword: "In the pursuit of a higher education, the students of the Daytona Beach Junior College have become temporary innkeepers. Although the facilities of an inn may not be entirely adequate for the purposes of education, we hope to prove that it is the students and faculty, not the façade of a building, that make up an institution of learning."

Dedication: "We gratefully dedicate this first Annual of the Daytona Beach Junior College to all those men and women who so generously gave their time and talents to pioneer the paths so these college doors could open."

Dr. James M. Synder, President—Comments: "It is seldom that a faculty and student body are privileged to start a new college together. In that respect we are fortunate. This college will be what we make it. Let's make it such that we will always be proud to be associated with it, and such that it will always reflect honorably upon us."

Administration:

Leon Fordman, Librarian

Dr. Owen Love, Director of Services

Dr. N. B. McMillian, Dean

Frederica Vincent, Receptionist and Switchboard Operator

Faculty:

Dr. Donaly Q. Butterworth, Music

Mary R. Connelly, English and Math

Dr. Merlin G. Cox, Social Science

Majorie Currin, Math and Psychology

Dr. Albert F. Dolloff, Physical Science and Physical Fitness

Harry Duffy Jr., Physical Science

Dorothea G. Foster, Guidance Counselor, Education

William R. Holton, Math and Philosophy

Lucy Shepard, Spanish

Frances D. Smith, English

Daniel B. Stout Jr., Math and Physical Science

Mariella D. Waite, Social Science

Index

A

Acker, Amy, 111

Adams, Eddie, 98

Adkins, Jameal, 109

Annual Multicultural Recruitment Day, 50

Askew, Reubin, 27

Arnold, Tami, 97

Atlanta University, 15

B

bachelor of applied science, 101, 111

Bailey Hall of Technology, 52

Baker, Paul, 15, 17, 27, 52, 67, 120, 121

Baliker, Paul, 53

Baylor, Chuck, 97

Beighle, J. Wayne, 72, 74, 120

Bell, Samuel, 46, 92

Bennett, Mary, 106, 120

Bergengren, Roy F., 14, 15, 18, 19, 23, 24, 27, 53, 54, 67, 119

Bert Fish Health Endowment, 56

Best, Julie, 106

Bethune-Cookman College, 24, 103

Blossom, J. Roland, 120

Blue Key Hall of Fame, 61

Bronson, Oswald, 103

Brown, Janet, 97

Brown, Laura, 106, 107

Brown, Leroy, 20

Brown, Sarah E., 120

Burden, Beatriz H., 120

Burns Elementary School, 45

Burt, David, 72, 74

Bush, Jeb, 102, 104

C

Callender, Lynnette J., 120

Campbell, Dale, 107

Campbell, Ralph, 20

Carlson, Eric, 111

Carroll, Charles, 60, 107

Casey, Josh, 111

Christiansen, Sylvia, 111

Clegg, John, 120

Clement, Fleurette, 111

Clement, Mercedes, 107

Coleman, Henry, Jr., 34, 42, 120

Collins, LeRoy, 44, 52, 67

Computing Commons, 49, 51, 82

Conway, Bill, 46

Creal, Charles, 15

Crowder, Robin, 51

D

Davidson, Herbert M., 51, 52, 120

Davis, David Lee, 35

Davis, Thomas F., 50

Davison, William H., 105, 120

Day, Philip R., Jr., 57, 58, 92, 119

DeLand campus, 44, 54, 56, 57, 74, 76, 78

Deltona campus, 44

Deltona Center, 46, 84

Desai, Pramila S., 120

District Board of Trustees, 15, 23, 27, 120

Dominican Republic, 5, 102

Dowdell, Letty Ann, 20

Dunlap, Ericka, 103

E

Edmunds, A. F., 9, 10

Edwards, James, 20

Ellison, Johnnie R., 20

Evens, Stacy, 29

F

Fathi, Fred, 107

Fernandez, Leonel, 102

Fish Memorial Hospital, 45

Flagler-Palm Coast campus, 44, 45, 86

Florida Community College System, 52

Floyd, Henry, 20

Ford, James, 120

Fox, Robert G., 38, 120

G

Gardner, James, 97, 120

Gautier, E. William, 120

Gillespie, Sally I., 72, 120

Goddard Center, 51, 52, 54, 98

Goddard, David, 54

Goddard, Jeanne M., 54

Golden, Yvonne S., 25

Graham, John, 120

Great Floridian Plaque, 24

Greene, J. Griffen, 15, 24, 26

Gregory, Amy, 97

Guthrie, John, 50, 51

H

Halifax Hospital, 13, 18

Hamby, Eileen, 111

Hannah, Terri, 111

Hansen, Patricia, 51

Harper, Ned, 108

Harvey, Ellery H., 120

Hawthorne, Kenneth B., 72, 74, 120

Herberger, Vanessa, 97

Hill, Katie, 97

Hold, Heather, 97

hotel-motel management, 18

Howington, Kaci, 106

Hosseini, Forough B., 105, 120

Hosseini, Mori, 54, 105

Hutchins, Sara, 107

I

InnKeeper, 16, 122

Instructional Television System, 16

Issena Hotel, 13, 16, 64

ITT Community Development Corporation, 45

J

Jackson, Dawn, 97

Janzen, Ashley, 106, 107

Johnson, Jim, 50

Jones, Heather, 97

Jose, Karen, 97

K

Karl, Mary Brennan, 6, 7, 9, 14, 51, 121

Kelly, Morris, 34

Kelly, Nella, 34

Kintz, Jennifer, 97

Kirk, Stacey, 97

Korwek, Alexander B., 120

L

Lacy, Ben W., Jr., 120

Lanier, Victoria, 97

Latimer, Charlene, 107

Lee, Linda, 50

Lemerand, L. Gale, 54, 55, 97, 120, 121

Lenholt, Eric, 14, 121

Lenssen, William, 120

Leonard, Albert J., III, 120

Lichtigman, Charles S., 120

Likes, Christopher K., 120

Ljungman, Ulnka, 106

Lombardo, Frank, 51, 107, 111

Lombardo, Roberto, 107

Lowery, Marvin Wade "Skip," 16, 122

M

Mainland High School, 6

Mallory, Peter E., 120

Mark, Mary Ellen, 98

Marsh, Tom, 97

Martin, Catheryn S., 120

Mary Karl Vocational School, 6, 9, 13, 98

Massey, Hal, 14

Mathis, Charles, 24

Matthews, Don, 108

Maxwell, Clark, 102

McCormick, Aubrey, 106

McKenney, John G., Jr., 120

McKinnon, Noah, Jr., 120

McLarnon, Brenda, 106

McLaughlin, Kristy, 106, 107

McMillian, N. B., 14, 119, 122

Megonegal, E. Russell, 120

Melton, Vickie, 107

Mercer, Ray L., 70, 120

Minority Recruitment Day, 50

Monte, Julia, 51

Monte, Meredith, 97

Moore, Misty, 97

Mortiere, Danielle, 97

Moses, Dora, 107

Mullane, Jess, 107

Municipal Stadium, 33

N

Nayar, Ram, 109

Nestor, James, 51

New Smyrna Beach-Edgewater campus, 45

New Smyrna Beach Senior High School, 45

Noble, Kathy, 51

O

Offiah, Sandra, 107

Olivari, Bill, 110

Opportunity School, 6

Overbey, Margaret, 107

P

Palm Beach Junior College, 7

Parks, Gordon, 98

Parrish, Lloyd, 111

Patrinelli, Henry, 9, 115

Paul, Mary Ann, 120

Peck, Edwin, Jr., 35

Perkins, Oliver L., 24

Peterson, Doug, 107

Peterson, Haywood, 111

Petrock, Joseph C., 29, 104-105, 117, 120

Phillips, Laura, 107

Phillips, Tiffany, 111

Pinkston-McDuffie, Joanne, 107

Polk, Charles H., 34, 41-44, 46, 72, 74, 119

Presswood, Kristy, 107

Primus, Bobbie J., 120

Princess Issena Hotel, 13, 16, 64

R

Ragsdale, Wendy, 87

Reynolds, Soli, 111

Rodriguez, Dipti, 111

Roland, Tiemey, 111

Roof, Joseph, 107

Roosevelt, Franklin Delano, 51

Roser, Richard, 120

Rowan, Roger, 88

Ruby, Fred, 50

Ruebel, Deah, 107

S

Sacks, Leonard M., 41, 70, 120

Sander, Theodor J., 120

Schildecker, William W., 54, 56, 120

Scullion, William, 120

Sessions-Robertson, Sandra, 107

Sharper, John, 20

Sharples, D. Kent, 5, 9, 97, 102-105, 107, 109-111, 116-117, 119

Shaul, Kayla, 106-107

Shoemaker, Merhl E., 41, 120

Shryock, Megan, 97

Sidor, Stanley, 109

Sieracki, Ali, 97

Smiley, John H., 9, 14, 19, 26, 67

Smith, Bernard, 24

Smith, Gregory, 105, 120

Smith, Walter L., 15

Smith-Hughes Act, 6, 98

Smolen, Alan, 120

Snyder, James M., 10, 13-14, 119

South campus, 51, 72, 75

South Volusia Center, 44-45

Southeast Museum of Photography, 98–99

Southern Association of Colleges and Schools, 23, 58, 101, 106, 111

Standard Man, 59

Starke, L. C., 120

Stetson University, 16

Sullivan, Margarita, 111

T

Termer, Grace, 111

Thigpen, Don, 47

Thompson, Paul, 61

Trein, Jessica, 106

U

University of Florida, 7, 11, 16, 51, 107

University of Michigan, 15

V

Valenti, Maria, 51

Van Dusen, Laurie, 107

VanWart, Christina, 107

Vela, Gary, 111

Vitale, Michael, 107

Volusia County Community College, 7, 11, 15, 20-21, 23-26, 69

Volusia County Vocational School, 6-7

Voorhees, Lisa, 61

W

Wadsworth, L. E., 120

Wadsworth, Wilhelmina, 120

Washington, Jacqueline D., 24

Watkins, Howell, 7

Wattenbarger, James L., 7, 9-10

Wattles, Kathleen, 51

WCEU-TV, 47

Webb, Julia, 24

Welch, Morgan, 15, 27, 120

West campus, 51

Wetherell, T. K., 41, 54

Wetherell, Thomas, 54

Wheelan, Belle, 106

Who's Who in American Community Colleges, 61

Williams, George R., Sr., 46, 72, 74, 120

Williams, Ozell, 20

Williams, Robert, 109

Wolf, Amy, 111

Wyatt, Lisa, 97

Author Biography Charles "Chip" Carroll

Charles "Chip" Carroll has worked at Daytona Beach Community College for thirty years. He has served under three of the College's presidents. He has taught at the College as well as held several administrative positions. Currently, he is senior vice president for Planning, Development, and Institutional Effectiveness. He holds an associate of science degree in respiratory care, two masters' degrees in psychology (educational and industrial/organizational), and a doctorate in higher education.

Daytona
Beach College